Original title:
Echoes of the Mystic Heart

Author: Sebastian Sarapuu
ISBN HARDBACK: 978-1-80565-073-7
ISBN PAPERBACK: 978-1-80565-276-2

The Tides of Inner Landscapes

In whispers soft the shadows play,
Upon the shores of dreams and clay.
With every wave that laps the sand,
A secret sigh, a guiding hand.

The moonlight dances, silver bright,
Upon the depths of endless night.
Where thoughts like tides in silence swell,
And weave their magic, hear their spell.

In twilight's grip, the heart can soar,
Through hidden paths to distant shore.
Each thought a star that lights the way,
In realms where night embraces day.

A journey deep, a quest untold,
In waters warm, and winds so bold.
To navigate the soul's own sea,
And find the truth that sets us free.

Through rolling waves, the spirit calls,
Echoes dance in shadowed halls.
Each tide a chance to dive anew,
In inner landscapes, brave and true.

Lullabies of the Forgotten Realm

In the hush of twilight's glow,
Whispers drift from long ago.
Secrets held in shadowed glen,
Softly sung by ancient men.

Moonlit paths through silver trees,
Rustle gently in the breeze.
Take the hand of fleeting night,
Dance with dreams until the light.

Echoes call from rivers deep,
Where the silent starlings weep.
Each forgotten lullaby,
Cradles hopes that never die.

Through the mist, a lantern's gleam,
Guides us to the heart of dream.
In this realm, both lost and found,
Magic spins around and 'round.

So close your eyes and heed the sound,
Of lullabies that wrap around.
Sleep now, child, drift far away,
To the land where shadows play.

Tides of Enchantment

Beneath the waves, the secrets lie,
In depths where moonlit glimmers sigh.
Whispers swirl in ocean's breath,
Promises made beyond all death.

Tides pull forth the dreams we chase,
Washing over with gentle grace.
Currents weave through time and space,
Guiding souls to their true place.

Mermaids sing of treasures lost,
In crystal caverns, shadows tossed.
Each note a spell, a magic thread,
Binding hearts with words unsaid.

Winds will carry tales that weave,
Stories spun for those who believe.
On sunset shores where silence rests,
Immortal dreams in fleeting quests.

Let the ocean's song enfold,
Embracing all the brave and bold.
With each wave, a new life starts,
An enchantment flowing through our hearts.

The Alchemy of Stillness

In the hush where time stands still,
Moments treasure calm and thrill.
Silken threads of thought entwined,
Whispers of the heart aligned.

Each breath taken, a golden hue,
Transforming pain to something new.
In the stillness, find the heart,
A canvas ready to restart.

Potions brewed from silence sweet,
On pathways where the shadows meet.
Alchemy of lost and found,
Where every silence makes a sound.

In this realm of quiet grace,
We discover our sacred space.
With each pause, the world unfolds,
Unveiling stories yet untold.

Let the stillness be your guide,
Where every tear may turn with pride.
In moments soft, the magic swells,
In the quiet, our spirit dwells.

Visions from the Dreamer's Edge

On the edge where dreams arise,
Beneath the soft, celestial skies.
Visions dance in silver light,
Guiding wanderers through the night.

In whispered tones, the secrets flow,
To hearts that yearn, and souls that glow.
Each dream a spark, each thought a fire,
Igniting hope, inspiring desire.

Across the canvas of the mind,
Painting futures yet to find.
With every heartbeat, every sigh,
New worlds are born, new spirits fly.

Here in twilight's gentle grace,
Imagination finds its place.
Let the dreams take wing and soar,
Into the realms where we explore.

So linger long on dreamer's edge,
Where magic calls and hearts allege.
In visions bright, we lose our dread,
On this threshold, dreams are fed.

Murals in the Cosmic Tapestry

In the night sky, stories unfold,
Galaxies painted in shades of gold.
Each star a whisper, a tale to tell,
Of cosmic wonders, enchanting and well.

Nebulae swirl in vibrant grace,
Time and space, a vast embrace.
Stardust drifts through the velvet night,
A canvas alive with luminous light.

Planets dance in a silent waltz,
Orbiting dreams, without faults.
Their colors vibrate, a radiant show,
In the tapestry cosmic, where wonders flow.

Threads of fate weave with care,
Whispering secrets in the air.
Murals of life, bright and grand,
Eternally linked, hand in hand.

Galaxies spiral, a gentle spin,
Reminders of all that lies within.
In the heart of night, we find our place,
A part of the mural, held in grace.

The Silent Dance of Starlight

In the twilight, shadows sway,
As starlight begins to play.
A gentle whisper fills the air,
The universe spins, crystal rare.

Celestial bodies twirl in prime,
A rhythm beyond the grasp of time.
With each glimmer, secrets unfold,
A dance of dreams, brave and bold.

Waves of light caress the night,
A silent song, pure delight.
In every shimmer, a message clear,
That love and hope are always near.

Chasing shadows, we find our way,
Guided by stars, come what may.
The moon serenades with silver beams,
While we wander through silent dreams.

In this cosmic swirl, we lose control,
Yet find the pieces that make us whole.
Together we dance in the depths of night,
Wrapped in the arms of starlit light.

Vignettes from the Edge of Reality

In the corners where whispers dwell,
Vignettes emerge, casting a spell.
Reality blurs, a soft embrace,
Fleeting moments, light as lace.

Time slips past in colors bright,
As dreams and echoes take their flight.
Scenes of wonder, surreal and grand,
A tapestry woven by unseen hands.

Fragments of thoughts in shadows play,
Dancing between the night and day.
Curiosities twinkle, alive and true,
In the veil that separates me from you.

Glimpses of stories, half-told,
Adventurers' hearts, brave and bold.
Each vignette sings a timeless song,
In the edge of reality, we belong.

Here, the world whispers in colors rare,
Inviting us gently, beyond despair.
Embracing the unknown, we learn to see,
The beauty in what we cannot be.

Symphony of the Soul's Journey

A symphony plays within the heart,
Each note a memory, never apart.
Echoes of laughter, shadows of tears,
Resonating softly, across the years.

With every heartbeat, stories arise,
Threads of silver beneath the skies.
Melodies intertwine, wild and free,
In the rhythm of life, we find the key.

The dance of the soul, a timeless affair,
Woven with love, nurtured with care.
Every turn tells a tale of its own,
In the silence of night, secrets are sown.

Notes of joy lifted high,
Floating like clouds in a summer sky.
And in the dark, where shadows may creep,
The symphony calls, a promise to keep.

Each soul a melody, unique and pure,
Together we rise, of this I'm sure.
In the grand performance, we play our part,
A symphony born from the depths of the heart.

Heartbeats Beyond the Horizon

In twilight's embrace, we sail anew,
With whispers of stars, the night sky grew.
Through shadows we wander, hand in hand,
Dreams weave their tales, across the land.

The horizon calls, a beacon of light,
With heartbeats synced, we chase the night.
Where wishes align and wishes mend,
In the dance of time, our souls extend.

Past fields of gold, where secrets lie,
Beneath starlit skies, our spirits fly.
With every pulse, the magic we spin,
A journey of love, where hope begins.

In moments fleeting, yet time stands still,
Echoes of laughter, a bittersweet thrill.
Through valleys of dreams, we shall explore,
Each heartbeat echoes, forevermore.

Mists of the Forgotten Dreamscape

In mists that swirl, the dreams reside,
Whispering secrets where shadows hide.
A realm of enchantment, lost to the day,
Where memories linger, and spirits play.

Through veils of memory, the past unfolds,
With tales of magic that time upholds.
In twilight's glow, the visions dance,
Inviting the weary to take a chance.

With each gentle sigh, the night breathes deep,
In this haunting place, we wander and weep.
For in the mists, the heart learns to yearn,
To rekindle the fires, and let them burn.

On pathways woven of silver and mist,
Forgotten dreams weave a fated twist.
With every heartbeat, a story we find,
In the echoes of time, our souls are entwined.

Incantations of the Soul's Voyage

Embarking on dreams that softly ignite,
With whispers of starlight, we take flight.
In the chambers of night, the shadows twist,
Invoking the magic, too sweet to resist.

Through twilight's embrace, our spirits soar,
In time's gentle grasp, we seek for more.
With every incantation, our hearts align,
In the tapestry of fate, your hand in mine.

The ocean of memory, vast and deep,
Within its embrace, our secrets keep.
With every wave, a promise renewed,
The song of our souls, forever construed.

We wander through realms where colors fade,
In the stillness of night, our fears are laid.
With the winds of change, we chase the sun,
In the symphony of life, we are one.

The Language of Lost Echoes

In the stillness of time, the echoes rise,
Whispering secrets through moonlit skies.
In shadows deep, where silence sings,
A language forgotten, the heartstrings bring.

Through the corridors of memory's hall,
We trace the footprints of those who fall.
With each gentle sigh, a story unfolds,
Of love and loss, in the silence it holds.

In the heart's quiet chamber, the echoes play,
Remnants of laughter, woven decay.
As stars twinkle bright, our spirits connect,
In the language of night, our souls reject.

The tapestry woven of dreams and despair,
Reminds us of moments, too precious to bear.
With every lost echo, a lesson is learned,
In the vaults of the night, our passions burn.

Chords of the Enigmatic Heart

In shadows deep where whispers dwell,
The heart will sing its secret spell.
A tune entwined with fate's own thread,
Awakening dreams from silence bred.

Each chord a memory softly spun,
Of battles fought and victories won.
In every beat, an echo clear,
The song of hope, dispelling fear.

Through twilight's veil and starlit sky,
The heart's refrain will never die.
For in the dark, the light will spark,
The chords of love, a timeless mark.

Let music guide the wayward soul,
Each note, a step towards the whole.
In harmony, our spirits rise,
To dance beneath the endless skies.

So listen close, for in the night,
The enigmatic heart takes flight.
With every pulse, a story told,
Of dreams beholden, brave and bold.

Flickering Flames of Eternity

In the hearth where embers gleam,
Flickering flames weave hopes and dreams.
As shadows dance in warm embrace,
Time stands still in this sacred space.

Each spark a wish, a whispered plea,
Igniting paths yet to be free.
In the glow, the past ignites,
A tapestry of starry nights.

Through trials faced, the fire grows,
An unyielding light that always flows.
In each flicker, a promise bright,
Eternity held in transient light.

From ashes rise new dreams each day,
In flames of passion, fears decay.
Together, we dance in light's embrace,
As flickering flames guide our pace.

In the heart of the night, we find our way,
Through flickering flames that never sway.
A circle complete, forever spun,
In the warmth of love, we are one.

Rhapsody of the Veiled Dawn

When morning breaks with gentle grace,
The rhapsody of dawn we trace.
In hues of gold and softest pink,
Awakens life and makes us think.

A symphony of light unfolds,
As twilight whispers secrets old.
Each note a promise, sweet and bright,
Embracing dreams that take to flight.

Through veils of mist, the sun will rise,
A wondrous sight to meet our eyes.
In nature's choir, we join the song,
Of life reborn, where we belong.

With every beam that spills and flows,
The rhapsody of dawn bestows.
A realm of magic, soft and warm,
Where hearts unite, and spirits swarm.

So let us greet the morning's light,
With open hearts and spirits bright.
For in the dawn's embrace we find,
A rhapsody that fills the mind.

A Dance with the Celestial Winds

Upon the hill where stars convene,
We sway and twirl in realms unseen.
The celestial winds call out our names,
In whispered songs, our hearts aflame.

With every breath, the cosmos swirls,
Our spirits lift, like twinkling pearls.
In moonlit glow, our shadows blend,
As time and space begin to bend.

The universe sings a lullaby,
A melody that cannot lie.
In perfect rhythm, we lose our fears,
With each soft note, the past disappears.

Together we dance, with wild delight,
Beneath the canvas of the night.
In harmony, the stars ignite,
As we find solace in the light.

So let the winds guide every turn,
In the celestial dance, our spirits burn.
For in this moment, we are free,
A dance eternal, you and me.

Ballads of the Hidden Dawn

In shadows deep where whispers play,
A hidden dawn begins the day.
With colors bright the world awakes,
From silken dreams, the heart it shakes.

The trees shall sway in morning light,
With creatures stirring in their flight.
Soft melodies of joy arise,
As nature sings beneath the skies.

The golden sun peeks through the leaves,
Awakening all that once believes.
In every heartbeat, life will sing,
As hope returns upon the wing.

So wander forth, ye brave of heart,
Embrace the dawn, new journeys start.
For hidden magic waits for thee,
In every breath, in every tree.

And when the stars bid night adieu,
The hidden dawn reveals the true.
With gentle grace it sweeps the land,
A ballad sung by nature's hand.

Illuminations from the Depths

In ocean's heart where secrets dwell,
The whispers weave a mystic spell.
Enchantments lost in tides of blue,
Illuminate the dark, the new.

With shimmering scales in sunlight's kiss,
The depths hold stories we can't miss.
For every wave a tale unfolds,
Of ancient worlds and treasures told.

Listen close, the sirens call,
In haunting echoes, we stand tall.
For in the depths, the truths reside,
Beneath the currents, dreams abide.

The seafoam dances, wild and free,
In every ripple, life's decree.
Illuminations from the deep,
Awake the wonders, soft and steep.

And when the night swallows the day,
The stars shall guide the lost astray.
For every heart that dares to dive,
Shall find the magic, still alive.

The Dreamweaver's Lament

In twilight's haze, where shadows creep,
A dreamweaver's heart begins to weep.
For threads of night are tangled tight,
In woven tales of lost delight.

Each whispered wish, a fading spark,
In memories hidden, buried dark.
Yet through the gloom, a lantern glows,
A hope that gently, softly grows.

But dreams can shatter, break and bend,
As echoes fade, and silence blends.
The tapestry of what was known,
Unravels softly, leaves us lone.

Yet in the night, our spirits soar,
For even loss can weave once more.
In every tear, a lesson learned,
In every pain, a fire burned.

So fear not, dear dreamer, hold on tight,
For dawn will break, and reveal light.
The dreamweaver's heart shall find its song,
In fragments lost, where we belong.

Stories Written on the Breeze

The wind whispers tales of yore,
In rustling leaves and ocean's roar.
Each sigh, a secret, each gust, a name,
With stories woven in nature's frame.

From mountain peaks to valleys wide,
The breeze carries dreams that cannot hide.
Of wanderers lost and sailors bold,
In every breeze, a new world told.

Listen close, for they will share,
Of joys and sorrows, love and care.
In every flutter, every sigh,
A history that will never die.

The breeze shall dance through fields of grain,
As echoes linger, joy and pain.
It carries laughter, whispers near,
A gentle touch for those who hear.

So cast your nets, dear hearts, and see,
The stories written on the breeze.
For every breath the wind imparts,
Holds the magic of many hearts.

Whispers of the Soul's Embrace

In twilight's hush, secrets unveil,
Dreams entwined in a silver trail.
Hearts breathe soft beneath the sigh,
An ethereal song that will not die.

Through whispered winds, a tale is spun,
Eclipsing shadows, two become one.
Fingers trace the paths of light,
In the embrace of the coming night.

With every heartbeat, magic we declare,
In the tender moments shared with care.
Lost in the melody of our own grace,
A journey blooms in the soul's embrace.

As dawn approaches, dreams take flight,
In the warmth of love, all feels right.
Guided by stars that shimmer with fate,
We dance together, hearts resonate.

Life's tapestry weaves a vibrant hue,
Each thread a promise, strong and true.
In this quiet space, souls ignite,
Forever bound within the light.

Shadows in the Moonlit Grove

Beneath the boughs where shadows dwell,
Whispers of secrets, a gentle spell.
Moonlight spills on the forest floor,
Echoing tales of those before.

The nightingale sings, soft and low,
Guiding the lost where wildflowers grow.
Each step taken, a heartbeat close,
Among the shadows, we find repose.

Ancient trees hold stories wide,
In their embrace, we must confide.
Ephemeral light through leaves does weave,
In the grove's hush, we dare to believe.

With every glance, the night unfolds,
Adventures whispered, the brave and bold.
In the moon's glow, our spirits rise,
A dance of shadows beneath starry skies.

As dawn approaches, a promise made,
In the grove's heart, love will not fade.
Together we roam where the wild things roam,
In the moonlit grove, we make our home.

Songs from the Winding Path

Along the path where wildflowers sway,
Sweet melodies linger and softly play.
Each note a story, a memory spun,
In the journey of hearts, the song's begun.

Waves of laughter rise with the sun,
Echoing joy from everyone.
With every step, the world awakes,
In the whispering breeze, the spirit shakes.

A bridge of dreams extends its hand,
Leading us forth to a promised land.
Through thickets dense and valleys low,
The songs of life in our hearts do flow.

Twists and turns may cause us to stray,
Yet every choice guides our way.
With courage held and love to cast,
We'll weave our future, spellbound and vast.

In twilight's glow, the path will gleam,
A tapestry woven from hope's great dream.
With every heartbeat, our journey unfolds,
In the songs of the winding path, we behold.

Secrets Beneath the Starlit Veil

Underneath the stars' soft glow,
Secrets murmur in the night's flow.
Each twinkling light a wish held dear,
In the stillness, our dreams draw near.

The night wraps us in its shadowed grace,
Time breathes slowly in this sacred space.
With gentle hands we weave our fate,
In the dance of dusk where hearts resonate.

Beneath the veil where mysteries swirl,
A tapestry of life begins to unfurl.
Stories of old emerge to share,
With starlit whispers floating in the air.

Through the darkness, hope lights the way,
Illuminating the paths where we play.
Every heartbeat carries a tale so grand,
In the cosmos' arms, we make our stand.

As dawn approaches, twilight fades,
The secrets linger in soft cascades.
In the sunlight's warmth, they intertwine,
Forever cherished, these moments divine.

Tapestry of Enchanted Stories

In the twilight's gentle fold,
Whispers weave tales of old.
Wizards and creatures take their flight,
Dancing stars in the velvet night.

Ancient spells in silken threads,
Promises made, where magic treads.
Timeless echoes softly call,
Binding hearts within their thrall.

On crescent moons, dear dreams reside,
In secret woods, where shadows hide.
With every stitch, a life is spun,
A universe in threads begun.

Through scattered pages, secrets gleam,
Casting forth a vibrant dream.
With every heartbeat, stories blend,
In the tapestry, lives transcend.

Fables whispered, lost in air,
Every child knows tales more rare.
Under stars that brightly insist,
We chase the dreams we dare to wish.

Rhythms of the Soulful Dawn

When the shadows kiss the night,
A soft promise, the morning light.
Golden beams through branches sway,
Awakening the soul's ballet.

Birds sing notes of pure delight,
Nature's choir, a splendid sight.
With each heartbeat, a new refrain,
Echoing hope in soft terrain.

Dew-kissed petals wake from sleep,
Whispers of secrets they will keep.
In every rustle, life begins,
The world awakens, dance of sins.

As the sun paints skies with gold,
Ancient stories waiting to unfold.
Every heartbeat, twirls and spins,
In the dawn where magic grins.

So let us rise with grace anew,
Embrace the day and all its hue.
For in the rhythms that we find,
Lies the melody of humankind.

The Shimmer of Ethereal Memories

In twilight's glow, a soft embrace,
A dance of shadows, time and space.
Moments linger, whispers sweet,
In the heart, where echoes meet.

Flickers of light, from days gone by,
Cascading dreams in the open sky.
Every sigh, a memory's spark,
Shining bright within the dark.

Lost in laughter, voices blend,
Crafting stories that never end.
As starlit nights weave tales anew,
In the shimmer, I find you too.

Fading glimpses, past times call,
Fragments caught like autumn's fall.
Yet in the quiet, we remain,
Bound by time, joy and pain.

In every heartbeat, every tear,
The ethereal whispers always near.
Together we dance through worn-out seams,
Woven forever, in fragile dreams.

The Heart's Algorhythm

Beneath the moon's enchanting glow,
The heart beats soft, a gentle flow.
In every thrum, a secret laid,
A symphony of love displayed.

Calculated paths intertwine,
In silent rhythms, souls align.
The pulse of worlds, a tender art,
Echoing the beats of the heart.

Time dances on a winding road,
Carrying whispers of love bestowed.
With every turn, our tales entwine,
In the heart's algorhythm, so divine.

Moments shared, in hushed delight,
An endless waltz through day and night.
In the silence, we find our fate,
The heart forever resonates.

So let our dreams ignite the sky,
With every heartbeat, we shall fly.
For in this rhythm, love we find,
A melody for heart and mind.

Whispers in the Veil

In the stillness of the night,
Whispers drift like gentle smoke,
Secrets carried on the breeze,
A soft song the stars invoke.

Through the shadows, voices weave,
Tales of old in silken thread,
Lost in echoes, hearts believe,
In every word, a dream is fed.

Dancing lights in the forest deep,
Stirring memories long confined,
In the silence, spells we keep,
Binding souls, entwined, aligned.

When the dawn begins to break,
Fleeting shades begin to fade,
Yet the whispers gently wake,
In the hearts where magic's laid.

Through the veil, the truth shall show,
Guiding seekers on their quest,
In the night, the shadows glow,
A dreamer's heart will find its rest.

Resonance of the Soul's Dream

In the cradle of the night,
Dreams take wing on silver light,
Echoes of a heartfelt wish,
Carried forth by moon's soft kiss.

Fleeting glimpses of the past,
Whispers touch the mind, so vast,
Threads of fate begin to weave,
Promises that hearts believe.

With each breath, the rhythm sways,
Time entwined in endless plays,
Singing softly in the void,
Souls united, never toyed.

As the dawn breaks into hue,
Songs of morning come anew,
A melody that softly hums,
The soul's dreams, forever drums.

In the dance of life we twine,
Echoes of the divine align,
Resonating, dreams take flight,
In the tapestry of light.

Shadows of Forgotten Cries

In the corners where shadows dwell,
Cries of silence weave a spell,
Echoes lost to fleeting time,
In the dark, they softly chime.

Whispers stir the ancient trees,
Tales of woe upon the breeze,
Forgotten names, rifts in the night,
A haunting song of faded light.

Beneath the moon's watchful gaze,
Shadows dance in ghostly haze,
Phantoms of a world once bright,
Carrying burdens wrapped in fright.

Yet within this mournful air,
Hope persists, a flicker rare,
From the depths of every sigh,
New beginnings scarce comply.

In the lull, the heart can see,
Shadows shift, the light shall be,
Resounding through the midnight cries,
A symphony beneath the skies.

Chants from the Celestial Depths

From the stars, a chorus beams,
Singing softly of our dreams,
In the light of ages past,
Celestial truths that hold us fast.

Whirling through the cosmic night,
Chants of wonder take their flight,
Rising tides of stardust song,
Binding souls where they belong.

In the cosmic cradle's embrace,
Whispers echo through the space,
Infinite in their design,
In the void, a spark divine.

Hear the echoes, feel the pull,
Hearts awakening, ever full,
In the depths where visions dwell,
Chants of love, a timeless swell.

Embrace the night, let the light flow,
Through the realms where spirits glow,
Chants from depths of the divine,
In unity, our hearts align.

Hues of the Celestial Canvas

In twilight's brush, the colors blend,
A tapestry of light, that seems to mend.
Stars whisper secrets, soft as a sigh,
Painting dreams in the vast, velvet sky.

Moonbeams dance on the shimmering deep,
Guardians of wishes, in silence they keep.
Constellations twinkle, a celestial choir,
Igniting the heavens with shimmering fire.

Crimson winds swirl in a cosmic waltz,
Spirits of starlight, a spectral pulse.
Each hue a story, a memory spun,
In the heart of the night, where all has begun.

Through galaxies' arms, the colors sail,
Echoes of beauty in every detail.
A canvas eternal, a masterpiece bold,
Dreamers traverse through shades of gold.

With every dawn, the hues may shift,
A reminder to cherish each moment's gift.
In the celestial realm, our spirits roam,
Forever intertwined, in the cosmos, our home.

Faint Drums in the Quiet Storm

Beneath the heavens, silence unfolds,
Whispers of nature, a story retold.
Faint drums echo, in rhythm they find,
The heart of the world, profoundly aligned.

Clouds gather softly, a shroud of grey,
Anticipation thrums, in a curious way.
Raindrops emerge, like tears from the sky,
In the quiet storm, where dreams learn to fly.

The pulse of the earth beats tender and low,
Nature's own heartbeat, a soft, steady flow.
Winds weave their secrets, between the trees,
Songs of the ancients carried with ease.

In the hush of the moment, magic ignites,
The world holds its breath, in wondrous flights.
As lightning writes verses in flashes of light,
The dance of the storm, both thrilling and bright.

When calm follows chaos, hope starts to bloom,
The shadows receding, dispelling all gloom.
Together we stand, with the earth as our guide,
In the faint drums' rhythm, our spirits abide.

The Song of Untold Journeys

With each step taken, a story we weave,
In the tapestry of life, where hearts believe.
The whispers of travelers, echoing wide,
In the melody of winds, our dreams coincide.

Mountains tall and valleys deep,
Hold the secrets of journeys we keep.
Rivers conspire with the stars above,
Guiding the wanderers, softly in love.

Every horizon, a promise anew,
Each shadow encountered, a chance to break through.
On roads less traveled, where wildflowers roam,
We find in the unknown, a piece of our home.

Candles flicker in the taverns of old,
As tales wrapped in laughter and valor unfold.
Through forests enchanted, and oceans wide,
Life's song of exploration, our hearts will abide.

So let us tread lightly, and dance with the breeze,
For each untold journey brings us to our knees.
In the echo of footsteps, a legacy spins,
In the song of tomorrow, the adventure begins.

Cadence of the Wandering Star

A lone star flickers, in the calm of the night,
With dreams in its glow, weaving fables of light.
Guiding the seekers, from worlds unknown,
In the cadence of silence, their paths are sown.

It waltzes through galaxies, gentle and free,
Painting the canvas of what was to be.
With each twinkle, a call to ignite,
The spark of adventure, in endless flight.

Amongst the shadows, where wishes take flight,
The wandering star sings of hope and delight.
It dances with comets, in cosmic embrace,
Writing our stories in celestial grace.

When darkness descends, and the veil is drawn,
The pulse of the universe beckons the dawn.
With lanterns aglow, and dreams held so dear,
We chase after stardust, with joy and with cheer.

So let us follow the light that we see,
For in the night's canvas, we are truly free.
In the cadence of journeys, both near and afar,
We find our own voices, with the wandering star.

The Hidden Garden of Dreams

In shadows deep where secrets lie,
A garden blooms beneath the sky.
With petals bright and whispers sweet,
Dreams awaken where lovers meet.

The moonlight dances on the leaves,
Weaving tales from what it weaves.
A gentle breeze, a lullaby,
In hidden paths where wishes fly.

Forgotten gates and ivy's grace,
In every corner, time must trace.
Beneath the boughs, the heart will soar,
In dreams unknown, we yearn for more.

The fragrance of a thousand nights,
Awaits the soul, ignites the sights.
Within this realm, the heart will claim,
Its deepest hopes, its purest flame.

So linger here, where dreams reside,
In nature's arms, let love abide.
For in this garden cloaked in haze,
The essence of our spirits plays.

Echoes in the Weaving Winds

Within the breath of whispered winds,
A melody that softly spins.
Echoes of laughter, faint and clear,
Calling us forth, drawing near.

The trees, they sway with ancient grace,
Each rustling leaf, a warm embrace.
The tales they tell of love and loss,
In every sigh, we feel the cross.

Beneath the stars, where shadows blend,
The gentle murmurs seem to send.
A string of hope, of longing hearts,
In every tune, where magic starts.

The weaving winds, they twist and twine,
A symphony of fate divine.
In harmony, our spirits sing,
Across the night, our dreams take wing.

So listen close, with open mind,
For in these echoes, truth we find.
The weaving winds, they guide our way,
As night transforms to break of day.

Reflections of the Heart's Desire

In quiet pools, reflections gleam,
Mirrors of the heart's own dream.
Each ripple stirs a thought so bright,
Beneath the depths of day and night.

The yearning flames that softly glow,
Illuminate what lies below.
Desires spoken, hopes untold,
In sacred whispers, bold yet cold.

We chase the essence of our fate,
In mirrored glass, we contemplate.
What lies within, we seek to find,
In gentle quests of heart and mind.

So let the waters guide our way,
As night gives birth to dawning day.
With open hearts, we will dance free,
In every drop, a memory.

For in these depths, the truth will rise,
Reflections clear before our eyes.
The heart's desire, a steadfast flame,
In stillness found, yet ever same.

The Pathway of Celestial Songs

Beneath the arch of starlit skies,
A pathway whispers, softly cries.
Celestial songs of ages past,
In every note, our dreams are cast.

The moonlight shines on golden trails,
Where magic flows and laughter sails.
In every step, a tale is spun,
A dance of shadows 'neath the sun.

The cosmos twirls, a dance divine,
As wanderers embrace the line.
With open arms, we greet the night,
And lose ourselves in pure delight.

Each star above, a guiding guide,
On pathways where our hopes abide.
With every heartbeat, songs arise,
Reflecting dreams that touch the skies.

So follow where the stardust leads,
In rhythm woven through our needs.
For on this path, we'll find our song,
In celestial embrace, we belong.

The Pulse of Hidden Realms

In shadows deep where whispers flow,
The heartbeat thunders, soft yet bold.
A dance of secrets, night aglow,
Beckoning tales from ages old.

Through ancient paths where magic weaves,
The echoes linger, dreams take flight.
Among the stars, the heart believes,
In hidden realms, purest light.

With every breath, a story starts,
In every beat, the unknown calls.
A tapestry of light and hearts,
Unfolding pride as darkness falls.

In moonlit glades where fairies sing,
The pulse of worlds begins to bloom.
A symphony, a wondrous fling,
In whispered hopes, dispelling gloom.

So let the magic guide our way,
With open hearts, we seek and find.
In hidden realms where spirits play,
A pulse of life, forever twined.

Threads of Starlit Visions

In twilight skies where dreams entwine,
Each thread a wish upon the night.
With shimmering spark and soft design,
We weave our hopes in silver light.

With every glance a pathway's made,
To distant lands where magic roams.
Through shadows cast and moonlight played,
A song of stars, our hearts find homes.

Beneath the veil of twinkling grace,
The universe sings sweet and clear.
In every flicker, gentle trace,
We gather visions, draw them near.

As constellations softly wink,
Our spirits rise, a cosmic dance.
In every heartbeat, love we think,
Threads of starlit dreams enhance.

So let us wander, free and bold,
Through realms where wishes spark and soar.
In threads of starlit visions told,
We find our place, forevermore.

Songs from the Silent Abyss

In depths unknown where shadows sleep,
A haunting melody takes flight.
From silent lands, the echoes creep,
Unveiling tales of dark and light.

With whispers soft like waves on stone,
The abyss sings a secret tune.
In every note, a truth is shown,
A lullaby beneath the moon.

Through icy depths and liquid night,
The songs of souls begin to rise.
In silent crests, we find our might,
As time unfurls before our eyes.

Each heartbeat echoes through the dark,
A symphony of dreams and fears.
In every silence, there's a spark,
A journey shared through joyful tears.

So let us dive into the deep,
With open hearts, embrace the sound.
In songs from the abyss, we leap,
And in that silence, life is found.

Lullabies of the Enchanted Woods

In dappled light where shadows play,
The lullabies of dusk arise.
With every breeze, the leaves sway,
A symphony beneath the skies.

Through whispering pines and ancient oaks,
The magic stirs, a soft embrace.
In hidden nooks, where laughter pokes,
The woods hold secrets, time and space.

With gentle hands, the fairies hum,
A rhythm sweet, both calm and bright.
In every heart, a beat will drum,
And dreams take wing to take to flight.

As twilight drapes its velvet shawl,
The creatures stir, the night begins.
Each lullaby, a calling call,
Where dreams ignite, and hope still spins.

So close your eyes, let spirits soar,
In enchanted woods, your heart will find.
With every song, you'll yearn for more,
A lullaby, forever kind.

Serendipity in the Midnight Forest

In shadows deep, where whispers lie,
The silver moon casts dreams awry.
Twilight beckons with a sigh,
A dance of leaves, the nightbirds fly.

Beneath the boughs of ancient trees,
A melody floats on gentle breeze.
Stars above, like eyes so wise,
Reveal the paths in twinkling guise.

A lantern glows, a secret path,
Embraced by magic's gentle wrath.
With courage held and heart ablaze,
I wander where the forest sways.

The owls hoot softly, a watchful tune,
While dewdrops glisten under the moon.
Each step unveils forgotten lore,
Serendipity opens a hidden door.

And as the night begins to fade,
The forest holds its tranquil shade.
In every breath, a promise higher,
Awakening the heart's true fire.

Pulse of the Soul's Journey

In a world of dreams and echoing sighs,
Every heartbeat is a whispering prize.
With courage stitched in a silken seam,
We chase the threads of a deeper dream.

Between the hills where shadows dance,
A fleeting chance, a timeless glance.
Each step we take, a story spun,
The pulse of life, forever begun.

In twilight's gleam, we trace our fate,
Each choice a key to the hopeful gate.
With every trial, our spirits soar,
Embracing all that we long for.

The wandering winds, a guiding light,
In the darkest hours, they shine so bright.
Through valleys low and mountains tall,
The pulse of our souls ignites us all.

So let us dance beneath wide skies,
With joyful hearts and dreaming eyes.
For in this journey, we are whole,
Finding magic in the pulse of our soul.

Enigmas of the Ethereal Light

In realms where shadows intertwine,
Ethereal light does brightly shine.
Whispers of secrets softly hum,
As ancient echoes bid us come.

Through veils of mist, illusions play,
Each flickering glow leads us astray.
A riddle wrapped in twilight's glow,
Invites the curious heart to know.

Beneath the gaze of silent stars,
We wander through the light's memoirs.
Each glimmer holds a fleeting chance,
To unravel destiny's dance.

In pathways lost and moments found,
Ethereal light beams all around.
A tapestry of dreams unfolds,
In every shimmer, new tales told.

So take a breath and close your eyes,
Embrace the wonder, let it rise.
For in the enigmas, truth takes flight,
Awakening souls to the ethereal light.

The Solace of Wandering Stars

When night descends in velvet deep,
The wandering stars begin to weep.
Each twinkle tells a tale of old,
Of dreams once whispered, brave and bold.

In the vast expanse, they gently sway,
Guiding lost wanderers on their way.
With every glow, a beacon bright,
They cradle hearts in the hush of night.

Through galaxies, our spirits soar,
Mapping the paths to distant shores.
In cosmic dance, we find our place,
The solace held in stellar grace.

With each pulse of light, a lullaby,
The universe hums, a soft goodbye.
In quiet moments, we understand,
The stars unite, a cosmic band.

So when you gaze up at the sky,
Let your heart weave with dreams that fly.
For in the night, our souls are far,
Connected forever to wandering stars.

Secret Melodies of the Night

In the cloak of darkness, whispers sing,
Beneath the stars, the shadows cling.
Λ gentle breeze with secrets flows,
As night unveils what daylight throws.

Rustling leaves in silken dance,
The world adorned in twilight's trance.
An owl hoots a timeless tale,
While dreams ride on the silvery veil.

Moonbeams play on dewy grass,
Echoing notes as moments pass.
With every sigh, the midnight sighs,
Inviting starlit lullabies.

Hidden tunes in shadows creep,
As weary souls drift off to sleep.
A symphony of whispers near,
In every heartbeat, night draws near.

Secrets linger where silence dwells,
In the nighttime's beckoning spells.
For those who listen, dreams take flight,
In the secret melodies of the night.

Reflections in the Still Water

By the water's edge, mirrors awake,
Cradling dreams that softly break.
Underneath the willow's sweep,
Ripples whisper, secrets deep.

Golden rays through branches weave,
In every pool, a tale to believe.
The gentle murmur of flowing years,
Echoes softly, laughter and tears.

Each glance reveals a hidden truth,
As time unveils the charm of youth.
While shadows dance, the past unfolds,
In still waters, a story told.

Stars above in crystal sky,
As night dips low, and dreams flutter by.
Reflections hold a fleeting glance,
Inviting hearts to take a chance.

From the depths, a lullaby springs,
The calm whispers of forgotten things.
In every ripple, life and fate,
In still waters, love resonates.

Murmurs of the Moonlit Path

On the trail where shadows sleep,
Whispers dance in secrets deep.
Guided by the silver light,
Through the realms of tranquil night.

Each step echoes with tales untold,
Of knights and myths in spirits bold.
Branches sway with ancient grace,
On this path of time and space.

Moonlit beams caress the ground,
In soft embraces, joys abound.
Every curve reveals a dream,
Where nothing's ever as it seems.

In the hush, a presence near,
The stories linger, crystal clear.
Murmurs hush the world around,
With every step, a magic found.

Wanderers, heed the lunar call,
As the night unveils it all.
In whispered tones, the path will share,
Murmurs of the moonlit air.

Harmonies of the Ancient Grove

In the heart of woods, where silence breathes,
Ancient songs weave through the leaves.
Timeless echoes in every bark,
Guardians of secrets, tall and stark.

Sunlight filters through emerald veil,
In the cool shade, lost stories trail.
The ground beneath, a rich embrace,
Where nature hums in sacred space.

Each rustling leaf tells tales of old,
Of mystic dreams and legends bold.
A chorus rises from mossy stone,
Where spirits roam and shadows moan.

Listen closely, hear the lore,
Of creatures wild and ages yore.
In every whisper, magic glows,
Harmonies of the ancient grove.

From roots entwined to branches high,
Life's melodies rise and sigh.
In nature's symphony, souls unite,
In the harmonies of day and night.

Dreams Beneath the Celestial Tide

In twilight's grasp, the stars awake,
Whispers of magic, the night shall stake.
Beneath the waves, a world unfolds,
Where dreams drift softly, stories told.

The moonbeams dance, a silver flight,
Guiding lost souls through shadowed night.
With each soft sigh, a wish takes sail,
On tides of hope, where hearts prevail.

The sea, a keeper of secrets vast,
Echoes of futures, present, past.
Every ripple, a promise made,
In the cool embrace of the waters' shade.

And as the dawn begins to break,
The night retreats, but dreams don't shake.
For in the depths of every sea,
Lies the spark of possibility.

So close your eyes, let visions rise,
With every star, a dream that flies.
Beneath the celestial tide so deep,
Awaits the mystery, yours to keep.

The Secret Map of a Wandering Heart

A map unfolds in starlit ink,
Each line a journey, a new link.
Wandering hearts bound by no shore,
Reveal themselves as they explore.

In valleys deep where shadows blend,
A compass of hope, on dreams depend.
Through whispering winds and rustling leaves,
The heart's true path is what it believes.

Every step a song, in soft refrain,
Guided by love through joy and pain.
With hidden treasures in every glance,
A secret map leads to a chance.

The stars conspire, the night ignites,
Illuminating paths with glowing lights.
In every wander, a piece to find,
The scattered fragments of the mind.

So let the heart set forth and roam,
For every journey finds its home.
In chapters written, the tale unfolds,
A secret map — a heart of gold.

Pulse of the Enigmatic Night

Underneath the arch of night,
The world pulsates with hidden light.
Each heartbeat echoes, soft and low,
In the velvet shadows, secrets grow.

The moon hangs bright, a watchful eye,
While mysteries dance and slowly sigh.
In corners dark, the whispers bloom,
Painting the air with tales of gloom.

Stars twinkle like thoughts half-spoken,
Promises made, yet often broken.
Each veil of night, a story spun,
A tapestry rich, where dreams are won.

Embrace the stillness, feel the beat,
As echoes linger, soft and sweet.
A pulse of wonder, strong and clear,
Awakens the magic drawing near.

So linger long in twilight's gaze,
Lose yourself in the night's soft maze.
For in every heartbeat, the night will prove,
The pulse of life is love's own groove.

Lament of the Celestial Being

In silence deep, a being weeps,
Their sorrow woven in cosmic leaps.
Stars weep with them, as they reflect,
The timeless ache of dreams unchecked.

Across the void where echoes hum,
A lamentation, soft and numb.
Each tear a star that longs to shine,
A celestial heart, lost in time.

The galaxies whisper their sweet refrain,
Of love and loss, of joy and pain.
A tapestry of light and dark,
The canvas where hope ignites a spark.

Yet in the sorrow, beauty blooms,
In shadows cast, the light consumes.
A dance of planets in silent flight,
Chasing the echoes of forgotten night.

So let the being's heart unfold,
Embrace the tales that night has told.
In every lament, a blissful grace,
For even sorrow finds its place.

Chasing the Celestial Whisper

In twilight's grace, we seek the glow,
Where echoes linger, soft and low.
A whisper dances on the breeze,
Entwined with secrets of the trees.

With starlit paths that guide our feet,
We follow shadows, shy and sweet.
Their stories swirl in moonlit air,
A tapestry beyond compare.

Through silver streams and mystic woods,
In hidden realms where friendship broods.
We chase the light, the shimmered song,
A promise that we both belong.

The night unfolds like velvet dreams,
With constellations, silken seams.
They lead us to the realms unknown,
A journey where our hearts have grown.

In every whisper, wonders gleam,
A realm of magic, hope, and dream.
We'll chase the stars, and hand in hand,
We'll write our tale upon the sand.

Mysteries of the Starry Night

Beneath the cloak of endless skies,
A canvas painted, nightbird flies.
Stars twinkle like the eyes of fate,
In shimmering hues, they softly wait.

A cool wind sings, a gentle sigh,
Revealing secrets by and by.
Each shimmering light, a tale untold,
Of wishes whispered, brave and bold.

The moon, a guardian, silver bright,
Illuminates the dark with light.
Its glow unveils the hidden ways,
Where dreams and shadows, softly play.

In constellations, stories weave,
Of ancient hearts that dared believe.
The stars align, a cosmic dance,
Inviting all to take a chance.

To walk beneath this vaulted dome,
Where every glance feels like home.
We'll delve into the night's embrace,
And find our way to that sacred place.

The Symphony of Elusive Dreams

In slumber's realm, where shadows weave,
A symphony of dreams believes.
Notes of wonder fill the air,
With whispers tender, soft, and rare.

A melody of hopes takes flight,
As stars compose the gentle night.
Each dream a story yet to hear,
A canvas bright, both bold and clear.

Through winding paths, we'll softly roam,
In echoes of a distant home.
The harmony of hearts will blend,
As magic lingers without end.

With every heartbeat, worlds collide,
In realms where all our fears reside.
Yet courage blooms like flowers bright,
Illuminated by starlit night.

So let us dance, though shadows call,
And trust the dreams that do enthrall.
For in this symphony of grace,
We'll find our journeys, time and space.

The Lantern of Forgotten Whispers

A lantern glows in twilight's haze,
Its flick'ring light, a silent praise.
Through forgotten paths, it softly leads,
To places where old magic breeds.

Whispers linger in the air,
Carried gently everywhere.
Each word a memory, faint and sweet,
That beckons us to pause, to meet.

In shadows deep, the stories play,
Of those who wandered, lost their way.
Yet in the dark, a heart can find,
A compass made of love entwined.

So let the lantern guide you near,
With every glow, dispelling fear.
In whispered tales, the past returns,
As hope within our spirit burns.

As night unfolds its velvet hue,
We'll light our way, just me and you.
For every whisper, every spark,
Can guide us home, through ages dark.

Serpent's Breath on Twilight's Edge

In whispers low, the shadows play,
A serpent coils, the twilight sway,
Beneath the stars, a secret kept,
Where dreams, like rivers, softly wept.

The moonlight flickers on cobblestones,
Ancient echoes in hushed tones,
A breath of magic in the air,
That lingers long, a sweet despair.

Each sigh a spell, each heartbeat reels,
In twilight's dance, the darkness steals,
Yet hope ignites with the dawn's embrace,
Transforming night into a chase.

With every step, the serpent glides,
Through realms unseen, where magic hides,
A pathway forged with tales untold,
As twilight dances, brave and bold.

So heed the call of whispered lore,
For every end opens a door,
To senses sharp, and hearts aglow,
As twilight's breath begins to flow.

Reverberations of the Timeless Heart

In shadows deep, a heartbeat thrums,
Where time stands still, the past becomes,
A tapestry of moments spun,
With threads of light, the dance begun.

Each echo rings of love's embrace,
In the stillness, we find our place,
A swirling mist of dreams misplaced,
Yet through the fog, we dare to race.

The timeless heart, it knows no bounds,
In whispered winds, a wisdom found,
As ages pass and seasons shift,
The core remains, a precious gift.

With every pulse, the world aligns,
In realms where fate and fortune twines,
A symphony of hopes and fears,
Resonating through the years.

So trust the beat that echoes near,
For in each thump, the truth is clear,
A dance of souls, a radiant chart,
In the reverberations of the heart.

Fables of the Wandering Spirit

In twilight's glow, the spirits roam,
Through whispered tales, they seek a home,
With every step, a story breathes,
Of lost adventures 'neath the eaves.

Through hidden paths, where shadows weave,
The wandering heart learns to believe,
In fables spun from ancient lore,
As echoes beckon evermore.

Beneath the stars, their laughter rings,
In realms where hope and wonder flings,
A dance of souls in moonlit grace,
Bound by the stars' eternal embrace.

Yet silence speaks in gentle tones,
With wisdom whispered through the stones,
In every footstep, truth immersed,
The wandering spirit, forever cursed.

So heed the call of every tale,
For in their depths, our hearts set sail,
In fables of the night's sweet trails,
Where wandering spirits weave their sails.

Tales Written in the Wind

On breezes soft, stories unfold,
In whispered tones, the secrets told,
From tree to tree, the voices glide,
Carving paths where dreams abide.

Each gust a brush of fate's design,
With every swirl, a heart will shine,
A tapestry of hopes unwound,
In nature's breath, our souls are found.

The wind, a scribe of ancient lore,
Penning tales forevermore,
Of love and loss, of joy and strife,
In every sigh, the pulse of life.

So walk the paths where echoes play,
And let the winds guide your way,
For in their arms, the world reveals,
The stories woven, the truth it feels.

Embrace the breeze that stirs the leaf,
For in that dance, we find relief,
In tales written where wild hearts bend,
As whispers soar and never end.

The Flicker of Hidden Truths

In shadows where whispers dwell,
Secrets dance, as stories tell.
A flicker glimmers in the night,
Truths emerge, trembling with light.

The moon, a sentinel so wise,
Guards the paths where mystery lies.
With each step, a tale unfolds,
In silent echoes, the brave behold.

The stars weave tapestries above,
Of longing, loss, and whispered love.
Beneath the veil of twilight's grace,
Hidden truths find their rightful place.

In realms where dreams and fears collide,
The flicker guides through the divide.
A lantern bright, through foggy seas,
Revealing what the heart believes.

So wander forth, let courage lead,
For in each heart, a hidden seed.
With every flicker, embrace the thrall,
Of truths that stir within us all.

Chronicles of the Endless Sky

Beneath the vast and endless blue,
A tapestry of dreams ensues.
Winds carry whispers of the stars,
In chronicles written from afar.

Time flows like rivers carved in stone,
Each moment a melody, all its own.
Clouds form castles, high and grand,
Holding secrets of the land.

The sun paints tales at break of dawn,
As shadows dance upon the lawn.
In twilight's kiss, the horizon glows,
While starlit paths await life's prose.

A skyward gaze ignites our fire,
With dreams unbound, we climb ever higher.
For in the stars, our hopes converge,
Guiding hearts on paths that emerge.

Chronicles woven in celestial light,
Illuminating shadows, igniting the night.
In the end, we find our way,
With every breath, we greet the day.

The Heartbeat of the Infinite

In silence deep, a pulse awakens,
The heartbeat of all that is unshaken.
With every thrum, the cosmos sighs,
Embracing dreams beneath endless skies.

Time ebbs and flows like ocean tides,
Carrying whispers where truth abides.
Each moment a spark in the grand design,
Threads of fate in patterns divine.

In the void where echoes leap,
The heartbeat resonates, a promise to keep.
With every breath, we weave and mend,
A life intertwined, with no end.

The stars pulse softly, a symphony bright,
Reminding us all of our inner light.
In every heartbeat, we find our place,
In the tapestry of time and space.

So listen closely to the rhythm's call,
For in that beat, we are one and all.
The infinite hums, a timeless tune,
In hearts united, beneath the moon.

Wisps of Wandering Intuition

Like morning mist that drifts on air,
Wisps of thought can vanish rare.
From depths unseen, they gently rise,
Guiding souls with whispered sighs.

In quiet moments, intuition speaks,
A gentle voice when the spirit seeks.
Through winding paths and hidden bends,
A compass true that never ends.

With every flutter, wisdom shows,
The heart's whisper, the mind's repose.
In serendipity's soft embrace,
We find our way, we find our place.

Trust the signs that life bestows,
In currents where fluid magic flows.
For in the chaos, clarity finds,
The hidden road that fate unwinds.

So let your spirit roam and play,
In wisps of thought that gently sway.
For intuition, like a tender friend,
Leads us onward, without end.

Reverberations of Lost Dreams

In shadows where the wishes fade,
Whispers dance on starlit glade.
Echoes linger in the mist,
Fading lights of what once kissed.

Each hope a feather, drifting low,
Carried by the silent flow.
Beneath the night, they softly sigh,
In twilight's arms, they gently lie.

Yet in the heart, a spark remains,
Where laughter mingles with the pains.
The dreams we've lost, the paths untrod,
Are woven still in the fabric of God.

Though time may fray, and shadows creep,
In secret corners, our wishes sleep.
Perhaps one day, with dawn's embrace,
We'll find those dreams, in light's warm grace.

So hold them close, those whispers small,
For hidden dreams can still enthrall.
In silence, they await the day,
When stars align, and lights will play.

Resonance in the Silent Night

The moon hangs low, a silver tune,
Beneath a sky of midnight's rune.
Stars murmur secrets, soft and sweet,
In shadows' arms, the stillness greets.

Whispers float on the gentle breeze,
Carried forth through ancient trees.
In silence vast, the heart does learn,
The echoes of the world, they yearn.

Each note a promise, softly spun,
In quiet corners, dreams undone.
The night unfolds like velvet deep,
Cradling stories that time shall keep.

Listen close to the cosmos' breath,
In every pause, there lies a depth.
For in the night, a lullaby,
Awaits the weary wanderer's sigh.

With every pulse and twinkling star,
The magic lingers, near yet far.
Resonance in the silent night,
Guides us home with gentle light.

Murmurs of the Ancient Spirit

In realms where shadows softly weep,
The ancient spirit stirs from sleep.
With echoes woven like a dream,
It whispers secrets, soft as cream.

Through forests deep, and mountains high,
The murmurs flow like a lullaby.
Each rustle speaks of times gone by,
And weaves a tale beneath the sky.

From stones of old, and rivers wide,
The spirit's voice cannot hide.
In every leaf, and every stone,
Lies wisdom etched in time alone.

Thus walk with care through sacred lands,
For ancient whispers hold your hands.
In darkness, light may often dwell,
In spirit's murmur, all is well.

So listen close, with heart attuned,
To wondrous truths and dreams resumed.
The ancient spirit, ever near,
Bears glimpses of what we hold dear.

The Heart's Hidden Symphony

Beneath the hush of life's sweet strain,
A melody plays through joy and pain.
In every heartbeat, a note unfolds,
A symphony of stories told.

Each breath a chord, both strong and light,
In shadows deep, and moments bright.
The heart composes, night and day,
A song that guides us on our way.

Harmony found in laughter's chime,
In tender moments, out of time.
The rhythm dances, wild and free,
In stillness, hear the melody.

In every love, in every tear,
The symphony swells, ever near.
Notes of the past, each hope and dream,
Weaving through life like a sunbeam.

So close your eyes, and feel the sound,
The heart's symphony, all around.
With every pulse, with every sigh,
A timeless song that cannot die.

The Twilight Portals of the Heart

In the hush of twilight's glow,
Whispers dance where secrets flow,
Portals open, dreams take flight,
Guiding souls through starry night.

Hearts entwined in gentle lore,
Beneath the sky, forevermore,
Memories weave like threads of gold,
In every heartbeat, stories told.

Casting shadows on the ground,
Love's soft echo wraps around,
Through the mist, a promise sways,
In twilight's grace, time gently stays.

With every sigh, the world unfurls,
Beneath the dance of lunar pearls,
A glimpse of fate within a glance,
A fleeting moment, sweet romance.

So linger here where dreams derive,
In twilight's arms, our spirits thrive,
For in these portals, hearts unite,
In endless realms of soft moonlight.

Harmonies of the Enchanted Spirit

In whispers soft, the spirits sing,
A melody of wondrous things,
Each note a tale of ages past,
In rhythms deep, forever cast.

Once in shadows, now in light,
Enchanted dreams take graceful flight,
Harmony flows through every tree,
Filling the air with mystery.

With starlit eyes, we chase the sound,
Our hearts are woven, tightly bound,
In nature's song, we find our place,
In every breath, a warm embrace.

Through moonlit glades and twilight's song,
We dance together, brave and strong,
For in this world of magic's art,
We find the truths that touch the heart.

So let us heed this spirit's call,
Embrace the rise and fall,
In every note, a spark ignites,
In harmony, our souls take flight.

Shadows of the Ethereal Embrace

In dusk's deep cloak, the shadows play,
Ethereal whispers float away,
An embrace of night hugs the sun,
In the silence, all is one.

Veils of twilight shroud the skies,
Dreams unfold in soft surprise,
In each shadow, truths are drawn,
By the gentle touch of dawn.

Within the dark, a light survives,
As ancient magic still contrives,
To weave the lines of fate and chance,
In shadows deep, we find our dance.

So close your eyes and feel the sway,
Of ethereal forces at play,
In silent depths, love finds its grace,
In every shadow, a warm embrace.

With every heartbeat, darkness yields,
To the shimmering light that shields,
In the magic that night brings,
Our hearts alight with ethereal wings.

The Essence of Forgotten Time

In quiet corners of the mind,
The essence of time is intertwined,
Memories linger, soft and sweet,
In echoes of hearts that used to beat.

Forgotten tales in whispers told,
Of timeless nights and days of gold,
Each moment cherished, slowly fades,
Yet in our dreams, that essence stays.

From dawn till dusk, the clock will chime,
Reminding us of the flow of time,
In gentle sighs, nostalgia creeps,
Awakening the soul that sleeps.

Through the passage that we roam,
In every journey, we find home,
For in our hearts, the essence lies,
A tapestry beneath the skies.

So treasure well each fleeting breath,
For in their depths, we conquer death,
The essence lives, forever bright,
In every shadow, in every light.

Ciphers of the Heart's Longing

In shadows cast by twilight's grace,
A heart concealed, a secret place.
Whispers haunt the evening air,
Longing blooms, a wish laid bare.

Each sigh a code, each glance a key,
Unlocking dreams that cannot be.
In every beat, a story spun,
In silence spoke, the lost and won.

Beneath the stars, they intertwine,
Two souls bound by fate's design.
Ciphers dance on threads of fate,
Each heartbeat echoes, never late.

Through tangled paths of time they roam,
In every yearn, they find their home.
Yet shadows linger, dark and stark,
Holding close the echoes of their spark.

But in the night, where dreams take wing,
The heart will always seek to sing.
In every wish, a truth will swell,
Of ciphers deep, where heartstrings dwell.

The Veil of Enigma

In moonlit halls of mystery's shroud,
A riddle wrapped both soft and loud.
Veils cascade like petals fall,
Whispers rise, a hidden call.

Enigmas swirl in dusky light,
Sowing dreams throughout the night.
Every glance, a question posed,
In shadowed glances, truth enclosed.

Each secret held in starlit skies,
Unraveled by the heart's soft sighs.
Tangled threads of fate align,
Revealing paths where destinies twine.

Yet signs are cloaked, in riddles spun,
The quest for truths has just begun.
With patience, time will unresign,
To bear the fruits of love's design.

So linger here, 'neath twilight's hand,
As secrets shift like grains of sand.
For in this dance of shadows cast,
Lies the promise of a spellbound past.

Melodies of the Whispering Moons

When evening falls, a song takes flight,
Beneath the gaze of soft moonlight.
Whispers weave through silken streams,
A lullaby that gently gleams.

The silver beams like fingers trace,
Each note a soft, enchanting embrace.
In twilight's breath, a symphony,
Of hopes and dreams that yearn to be.

Each star a chord, each sigh a tune,
Together play beneath the moon.
With every strum, a heart will soar,
In melodies that hush and roar.

Yet echoes linger, soft and sweet,
Through tangled paths where lovers meet.
The night transforms each whispered plea,
Into a dance of harmony.

So listen close, as shadows blend,
For love's sweet song shall never end.
In every heartbeat, in every glance,
Lie melodies that dare to dance.

The Dance of Fading Echoes

Through halls where silent memories tread,
A dance unfolds in shades of red.
With every step, a story told,
Of fleeting dreams and hearts so bold.

Each echo rings in twilight's breath,
Shadows waltz with whispers of death.
In circles cast by hands of fate,
They spin, entwined, they simply wait.

In fleeting glances, love turns pale,
A bittersweet, unending tale.
Yet in the dusk, a fire glows,
As every fading moment shows.

Through realms of time where spirits play,
They dance beneath the moon's soft sway.
With every pulse, the echoes call,
In the quiet night, they rise and fall.

So twirl in dreams, though shadows loom,
For every dusk will birth a bloom.
In fading echoes, find your song,
In the dance of life, you shall belong.